PROFIT PROWESS

Strategies for Economic Triumph

By

SMITH E. HECTOR

COPYRIGHT

PREFACE

Welcome to the world of economic triumph and profit prowess. As we embark on this journey together, I am excited to introduce you to the pages of "Profit Prowess: Strategies for Economic Triumph." This book is not just a compilation of theories; it is a roadmap, a guide crafted through years of observation, analysis, and the collective wisdom of successful entrepreneurs and business leaders.

The inspiration for this book stems from a deep-rooted curiosity about what sets successful businesses apart. Why do some enterprises thrive while others falter? What are the strategies that propel a business toward economic triumph? These questions fueled my exploration into the intricate dynamics of profit generation and economic success.

In the first chapters, we delve into the fundamentals, understanding the economic landscape and the dynamics that shape it. From market analysis to recognizing the subtle yet powerful economic factors, we lay the groundwork for a comprehensive understanding of the environment in which businesses operate. In doing so, we set the stage for cultivating profit prowess.

A resilient business model is the cornerstone of economic triumph. Section II guides you through the process of crafting a business plan that not only withstands challenges but also thrives in diverse market conditions. We explore the art of identifying niche opportunities and how a well-defined focus can be a catalyst for sustained profitability.

Profitability is not just about revenue; it's about how you manage and allocate resources. Section III takes a deep dive into financial management strategies. From efficient budgeting to maximizing revenue streams, we uncover the financial intricacies that separate successful ventures from the rest.

In the age of digital dominance, marketing is a pivotal force driving economic success. Section IV is dedicated to unraveling the secrets of creating a strong brand presence and leveraging digital marketing tools. We explore how successful businesses master the art of marketing to not only survive but thrive in competitive markets.

The business landscape is ever-evolving, and those who embrace change are the ones who lead. Section

V discusses the importance of innovation, adaptability, and effective leadership in the pursuit of profit prowess. We examine case studies of businesses that navigated technological advancements and economic uncertainties with finesse.

Section VI presents a series of case studies, offering an in-depth look at successful businesses and the strategies that propelled them to economic triumph. By dissecting these triumphs, we extract valuable lessons that can be applied to diverse industries and business scales.

No journey is without challenges. Section VII acknowledges the common obstacles to economic triumph and provides proven solutions and strategies. It's a guide for overcoming hurdles and turning challenges into opportunities for growth.

The world is in a perpetual state of change, and the ability to anticipate and adapt to future trends is a hallmark of successful businesses. Section VIII explores emerging opportunities in the global economy and offers insights on how to position your business for success in the years to come.

As you read through these pages, I invite you to actively engage with the content. Reflect on your own experiences, challenge your assumptions, and consider how the principles shared here can be applied in your unique business context. This book is not a one-size-fits-all solution but rather a flexible guide that encourages strategic thinking and adaptability.

In conclusion, "Profit Prowess: Strategies for Economic Triumph" is more than a book; it's a companion on your journey to business success. Whether you're an aspiring entrepreneur, a seasoned business leader, or someone passionate about understanding the intricacies of economic triumph, I hope you find this exploration both insightful and actionable.

Here's to your journey towards profit prowess and economic triumph.

Happy reading!

Smith E. Hector

DEDICATION

To the Readers,

This book is dedicated to each of you who embark on the journey of economic triumph. In the vast expanse of economic landscapes, you are the architects of change, the innovators of tomorrow, and the catalysts for progress. Your curiosity, resilience, and commitment to growth inspire the narrative within these pages.

May this book serve as a guiding light, offering insights, strategies, and encouragement as you navigate the complexities of economic endeavors. In your pursuit of triumph, may you find not just financial success but also fulfillment, purpose, and the satisfaction of making a positive impact.

Here's to the readers, the dreamers, and the doers. Your dedication to shaping a brighter economic future fuels the essence of this book. May your journey be filled with learning, growth, and the realization of your most ambitious aspirations.

With gratitude and best wishes,

Smith E. Hector

TABLE OF CONTENTS

INTRODUCTION

Overview of Economic Success

Economic success is a multifaceted concept that extends beyond the traditional notion of financial prosperity. It encapsulates a broader spectrum of achievements, reflecting the capacity of businesses and economies to thrive, adapt, and create sustainable value. As we navigate the intricate landscape of economic success, it becomes evident that it is not merely a destination but a continuous journey shaped by strategic decisions, effective management, and the ability to respond to an ever-evolving global environment.

At its core, economic success is intricately tied to a deep understanding of market dynamics. Businesses that grasp the nuances of market trends, consumer behaviors, and industry shifts are better positioned to not only survive but to excel. This comprehension forms the foundation upon which strategic decisions are made, enabling businesses to proactively identify opportunities and navigate challenges. Economic success, in this sense, begins with a keen awareness of the external factors that influence the business landscape.

A robust business model is a linchpin of economic success. This model serves as a blueprint for how a company creates, delivers, and captures value. It goes beyond the surface-level aspects of products and services, delving into the intricacies of operational efficiency, scalability, and adaptability. Crafting a resilient business model involves a strategic alignment of resources, capabilities, and market needs. Successful enterprises recognize that a well-defined and flexible model is not only a defensive mechanism against uncertainties but also a proactive tool for growth.

Financial management emerges as a pivotal aspect of economic success. It is not merely about generating revenue but entails a judicious allocation and utilization of resources. Efficient budgeting, strategic investment, and a focus on maximizing revenue streams contribute to a healthy financial ecosystem within a business. Sound financial practices not only ensure short-term stability but also lay the groundwork for long-term sustainability and growth.

In the contemporary landscape dominated by technological advancements and digital connectivity, marketing mastery is indispensable for economic success. Creating a strong brand presence, understanding the intricacies of consumer engagement, and leveraging digital tools are essential components of a successful marketing strategy. Businesses that can effectively communicate their value proposition, build customer loyalty, and adapt to evolving marketing channels are better positioned to stand out in competitive markets.

The ability to innovate and adapt is a hallmark of economically successful entities. In an era characterized by rapid technological advancements and unpredictable market shifts, businesses must embrace change rather than resist it. Innovation, whether in products, processes, or business models, becomes a catalyst for growth. Moreover, adaptability is crucial for navigating uncertainties and disruptions. Economic success is often intertwined with a company's capacity to foresee trends, pivot when necessary, and seize emerging opportunities.

Leadership plays a pivotal role in shaping economic success. Effective leaders navigate their teams through complexities, make informed decisions, and foster a culture of continuous improvement. Leadership extends beyond individual brilliance; it involves cultivating high-performing teams, fostering innovation, and instilling a shared vision. Businesses led by leaders who inspire, empower, and lead by example are more likely to achieve enduring economic success.

Examining case studies of economic triumphs provides valuable insights into the practical application of strategies and principles. Real-world examples showcase how businesses have overcome challenges, leveraged opportunities, and executed successful strategies. By dissecting these cases, readers can glean actionable lessons that are applicable across diverse industries and business scales.

Challenges are inevitable on the path to economic success. Acknowledging and addressing common obstacles is a crucial aspect of resilience. Section VII of this exploration delves into the obstacles businesses often encounter and provides proven solutions and strategies. It serves as a guide for not just overcoming hurdles but leveraging challenges as opportunities for growth and improvement.

Anticipating future trends is essential for sustained economic success. Section VIII explores emerging opportunities in the global economy and offers insights on positioning businesses for success in the years to come. Businesses that can foresee and adapt to future trends are better equipped to navigate evolving market dynamics and maintain a competitive edge.

As readers engage with the content of this exploration, it is an invitation to reflect on personal experiences, challenge assumptions, and consider the applicability of the principles discussed. This book is not a rigid doctrine but a flexible guide that encourages strategic thinking, adaptability, and continuous improvement. Economic success is a dynamic pursuit that demands an active and thoughtful engagement with the principles and strategies presented.

In conclusion, "Profit Prowess: Strategies for Economic Triumph" is more than a compilation of theories; it is a comprehensive guide to navigating the complexities of economic success. Whether you are an aspiring entrepreneur, a seasoned business leader, or someone fascinated by the dynamics of economic triumph, this exploration aims to provide both insightful perspectives and actionable strategies.

Importance of Profit Prowess in Business

Profit prowess is not merely a financial metric but a strategic imperative that underscores the vitality of businesses in the competitive landscape. It goes beyond the simplistic pursuit of revenue generation, encompassing a holistic approach to financial management, operational efficiency, and sustained growth. Understanding the importance of profit prowess is fundamental for businesses aiming not only to survive but to thrive and make a meaningful impact.

At its core, profit prowess is a reflection of a company's ability to efficiently convert inputs into outputs, creating a surplus that can be reinvested for future growth. Profitability is a key indicator of financial health and resilience. Businesses that consistently generate profits are better equipped to weather economic downturns, navigate uncertainties, and invest in innovation and expansion.

The significance of profit prowess is heightened in the context of resource allocation. Profits provide the necessary fuel for reinvestment in areas such as research and development, technology upgrades, employee training, and market expansion. This, in turn, fosters a cycle of continuous improvement, innovation, and adaptability – essential components for long-term success in dynamic markets.

Moreover, profitability is integral to attracting investors and securing capital for strategic initiatives. Investors are naturally drawn to businesses that demonstrate not only a track record of profitability but also a clear vision for sustainable growth. Profit prowess enhances a company's credibility and ability to access funding, allowing it to capitalize on emerging opportunities and navigate challenges with financial resilience.

From an operational perspective, profit prowess influences decision-making at every level of an organization. It encourages a focus on cost-effectiveness, efficiency, and value creation. Businesses that prioritize profit prowess are more likely to implement rigorous financial management practices, optimize operational processes, and strategically allocate resources, resulting in a lean and agile organizational structure.

Employee engagement and satisfaction are also closely tied to a company's financial success. A profitable business is better positioned to invest in employee development, competitive compensation, and a positive work environment. This, in turn, fosters a motivated and committed workforce, contributing to increased productivity and innovation – factors that are crucial for maintaining a competitive edge.

In the broader economic context, businesses with profit prowess play a pivotal role in job creation and community development. Sustainable profits enable companies to expand operations, hire skilled professionals, and contribute to the overall economic well-being of the communities in which they operate. By being profitable, businesses become engines of economic growth, stimulating both local and global economies.

Furthermore, profit prowess is a testament to a company's ability to deliver value to its customers. Sustainable profitability is often a reflection of customer satisfaction, loyalty, and effective market positioning. Businesses that consistently meet or exceed customer expectations are likely to enjoy repeat business, positive word-of-mouth, and a competitive advantage in the market.

In conclusion, the importance of profit prowess in business cannot be overstated. It is a strategic imperative that extends beyond financial metrics, influencing operational efficiency, employee satisfaction, investor confidence, and community impact. Profitability is not a standalone goal but a dynamic force that enables businesses to innovate, adapt, and contribute meaningfully to the economic landscape. As businesses navigate the complexities of the modern market, cultivating and sustaining profit prowess emerges as a foundational element for enduring success.

CHAPTER 1: Understanding Economic Dynamics

Market Analysis and Trends

Market analysis is the cornerstone of strategic decision-making for businesses operating in today's dynamic economy. This practice involves a systematic exploration of the various factors influencing supply and demand within specific industries or market segments. By evaluating the overall economic environment, regulatory landscape, and competitive field, businesses gain valuable insights that inform key decisions related to market entry, expansion, and adaptation to changing conditions.

Understanding consumer behavior and preferences is a central component of effective market analysis. Beyond assessing what consumers purchase, businesses delve into the intricacies of why and how consumers make purchasing decisions. Analyzing demographic data, psychographics, and cultural factors allows businesses to tailor their offerings and marketing strategies to align with consumer expectations.

In tandem with consumer insights, businesses engage in continuous monitoring of industry trends and technological advancements. This forward-looking approach enables companies to anticipate shifts in the market, capitalize on emerging opportunities, and foster innovation. Staying abreast of the competitive landscape is equally vital, involving a thorough examination of competitors' strengths, weaknesses, market share, pricing strategies, and unique value propositions.

The SWOT analysis, a comprehensive evaluation of Strengths, Weaknesses, Opportunities, and Threats, is a valuable tool within market analysis. By systematically assessing internal and external factors, businesses can develop strategic roadmaps that inform decision-making, highlight areas for improvement, and identify potential areas of growth.

In an interconnected global economy, businesses must also consider broader economic trends. Factors such as inflation rates, exchange rates, and geopolitical events can influence market conditions. An awareness of these macroeconomic trends is essential for risk mitigation and strategic planning, particularly for businesses operating across multiple regions.

The era of big data has revolutionized market analysis, providing businesses with unprecedented access to information. Leveraging data analytics allows businesses to derive actionable insights from vast datasets, aiding in more informed decision-making. This data-driven approach enables businesses to tailor their strategies based on real-time information and trends.

However, market analysis is not a one-time effort but an ongoing process. Successful businesses cultivate a culture of adaptability and agility, continuously monitoring market trends and adjusting strategies accordingly. This iterative approach allows businesses to respond promptly to changing consumer behaviors, technological advancements, and competitive pressures.

In conclusion, market analysis and trend identification are indispensable for strategic business planning. By investing time and resources in understanding market dynamics, consumer behavior, and industry trends, businesses position themselves not only to survive but to thrive in the face of change. As markets evolve, businesses that prioritize comprehensive market analysis demonstrate the resilience and foresight necessary for enduring success.

Economic Factors Influencing Profit

The profitability of a business is intricately woven into the fabric of various economic factors that define the broader financial landscape. One of the foundational elements is the interplay of supply and demand dynamics. The delicate balance between the availability of goods and services and consumer demand often determines the pricing structure, directly impacting profit margins. Imbalances in this equilibrium can either bolster or hinder a company's ability to generate profits.

Fluctuations in the general price levels of goods and services, known as inflation or deflation, present significant challenges and opportunities for businesses. Inflationary pressures can increase the costs of production and operational expenses, thereby affecting overall profitability. Conversely, deflationary trends may lead to reduced consumer spending, posing challenges for revenue generation. The delicate dance between these economic forces requires businesses to adopt strategies that navigate changing price dynamics.

Interest rates, set by central banks, represent another critical economic factor influencing profits. Higher interest rates can increase the cost of borrowing, impacting both investment decisions and the overall financial health of a business.

Conversely, lower interest rates can make borrowing more affordable, potentially stimulating economic activity and, consequently, profit growth. Businesses must remain attuned to these interest rate fluctuations to make informed financial decisions that align with their long-term profitability goals.

For businesses engaged in international trade, fluctuations in currency exchange rates constitute a pivotal economic factor influencing profits. Changes in exchange rates can directly impact the cost of imports and exports, influencing the competitiveness of products in the global market. Managing these currency-related risks is crucial for maintaining and optimizing profitability, especially for companies operating in diverse economic environments.

Economic cycles of growth and recession have a profound impact on business profits. During periods of economic upswing, increased consumer spending tends to contribute to higher revenues. However, during recessions, consumer spending contracts pose challenges for businesses to maintain profit levels. Navigating these economic ebbs and flows requires a strategic approach that accounts for both short-term adjustments and long-term resilience.

The regulatory environment, shaped by government policies, taxation, and trade agreements, is an economic factor with direct implications for business operations and profitability. Changes in regulations can impact costs, market access, and compliance requirements, requiring businesses to adapt swiftly to remain profitable. Staying informed and proactive in responding to evolving regulatory landscapes is a crucial aspect of managing profitability.

Furthermore, technological advancements represent both a challenge and an opportunity for business profitability. Companies that embrace and integrate technological innovations can enhance operational efficiency, reduce costs, and gain a competitive edge. Conversely, businesses slow to adapt may find themselves at a disadvantage, impacting their ability to generate profits in the long run. The pace of technological change demands a proactive stance from businesses seeking sustained profitability.

Consumer confidence, reflecting the sentiment of individuals, is a key economic factor impacting profits. High levels of consumer confidence often correlate with increased spending, positively affecting business revenues. Conversely, low consumer confidence may lead to decreased spending, affecting the ability of businesses to generate profits. Understanding and responding to consumer sentiment are crucial aspects of maintaining a healthy revenue stream.

On the global stage, economic conditions in major economies can have a ripple effect, influencing commodity prices, supply chains, and demand for goods and services. For businesses operating internationally, these global economic conditions can significantly impact profitability. A comprehensive understanding of these interconnected economic forces is vital for businesses with a global footprint.

Labor market conditions, including the availability and cost of labor, play a critical role in shaping business profitability. Tight labor markets may lead to increased wages, impacting operational costs. Additionally, a skilled and motivated workforce can contribute to increased productivity, positively influencing overall business profitability. Striking the right balance in managing labor-related costs and fostering a conducive working environment is essential for long-term profitability.

In navigating this complex interplay of economic factors, businesses require more than just financial acumen; they need a keen awareness, adaptability, and strategic decision-making. The ability to anticipate, respond to, and capitalize on these economic forces is the hallmark of businesses that not only survive but thrive in dynamic and ever-changing economic landscapes. As economic factors continue to evolve, the pursuit of profitability becomes an ongoing journey that demands resilience, foresight, and a commitment to excellence.

CHAPTER 2: Developing a Robust Business Model

Crafting a Resilient Business Plan

Crafting a resilient business plan is a strategic endeavor that necessitates a comprehensive approach to ensure the long-term success and adaptability of your venture. The process begins with a thorough market analysis, delving into industry trends, consumer behaviors, and potential challenges. This foundational understanding allows your business plan to be rooted in the current realities of the market, providing a robust starting point for strategic decision-making.

At the heart of your business plan lies the clear articulation of your value proposition. Define what sets your business apart, how it precisely addresses customer needs, and why consumers should choose your products or services. This distinctive proposition not only serves as a marketing tool but also acts as a strategic anchor during market fluctuations, helping your business maintain a competitive edge.

Risk assessment and mitigation strategies form a critical aspect of resilience. Anticipate potential risks that could impact your business, whether they stem from supply chain disruptions, regulatory changes, or economic downturns. A resilient business plan not only identifies these risks but also outlines proactive measures to navigate challenges, ensuring that your business can weather storms and emerge stronger on the other side.

Diversification strategies contribute significantly to resilience. Explore opportunities to diversify your product or service offerings, customer base, and revenue streams. By spreading your business across multiple areas, you mitigate the impact of fluctuations in specific markets or industries, creating a more stable and adaptable business model.

Financial prudence is paramount in a resilient business plan. Develop a realistic and conservative financial plan, considering various scenarios, including adverse conditions. Establish contingency funds to navigate unexpected challenges without compromising the core operations of the business. This financial foresight provides a buffer against uncertainties, allowing your business to maintain stability even in challenging economic climates.

Scalability and flexibility are key considerations in crafting a resilient business plan. Design your operations with scalability in mind, ensuring that your business can efficiently scale operations based on demand. Flexibility in adapting to changing circumstances is equally important, allowing your business to pivot when necessary and respond effectively to evolving market dynamics.

The integration of technology catalyzes resilience. Explore ways to incorporate technology into your operations to enhance efficiency, streamline processes, and stay competitive. Technology not only improves operational effectiveness but also provides valuable data-driven insights, enabling your business to make informed and strategic decisions.

Sustainability practices contribute not only to ethical considerations but also to long-term resilience. Emphasize environmentally friendly practices and social responsibility. A commitment to sustainability not only aligns with evolving consumer values but also positions your business as one that is forward-thinking and adaptable to changing societal expectations.

Contingency planning is a critical component of resilience. Develop well-defined contingency plans for critical aspects of your business, including crisis communication strategies, alternative suppliers, and emergency response plans. Having these measures in place ensures a more agile and responsive business in times of uncertainty.

Continuous learning and adaptation are fundamental to resilience. Foster a culture that values ongoing learning and regularly reassesses market dynamics, industry trends, and internal operations. This adaptability ensures that your business plan remains relevant and effective in the face of evolving challenges and opportunities.

Strong leadership qualities are essential in building resilience. Cultivate leadership that emphasizes adaptability, effective communication, and strategic decision-making during challenging times. Additionally, invest in team development to ensure that your staff is equipped with the skills and mindset necessary to navigate uncertainties collaboratively.

In conclusion, a resilient business plan is a dynamic roadmap that not only outlines the path to success but also equips your business to withstand and thrive amid uncertainties. By integrating thorough analysis, risk mitigation strategies, and a commitment to adaptability, you lay the foundation for a business that can navigate challenges, seize opportunities, and emerge stronger on the other side.

Identifying Niche Opportunities

Identifying niche opportunities is a strategic process that involves recognizing unmet needs or underserved segments within a market. Successfully identifying and capitalizing on niche opportunities can give a business a competitive edge and open up new avenues for growth. Here are key considerations for identifying niche opportunities:

1. Market Research:
Conduct thorough market research to understand current trends, consumer behaviors, and gaps in the market. Analyze existing products or services to identify areas where there may be unmet needs or room for improvement.

2. Target Audience Analysis:
Define and understand your target audience. Identify specific demographics, preferences, and pain points. By intimately knowing your potential

customers, you can pinpoint niche opportunities that directly address their unique requirements.

3. Emerging Trends:

Stay abreast of emerging trends in your industry. Monitor technological advancements, shifts in consumer behavior, and changes in regulations that might create new opportunities. Being proactive in identifying and adapting to emerging trends positions your business for success in niche markets.

4. Competitor Analysis:

Analyze your competitors to identify gaps in their offerings or areas where they may be underserving certain customer segments. Understanding the strengths and weaknesses of competitors can reveal potential niche spaces for your business to occupy.

5. Customer Feedback:

Listen to customer feedback attentively. Whether through surveys, reviews, or direct communication, customer insights can highlight areas where existing products or services fall short. Addressing these pain points can lead to niche opportunities that cater to specific customer needs.

6. Unconventional Perspectives:

Challenge conventional wisdom and consider unconventional perspectives. Niche opportunities often arise from thinking outside the box and identifying solutions or products that may not conform to traditional market norms.

7. Industry Networking:

Engage with industry networks and attend relevant events. Networking can provide valuable insights into emerging opportunities and market gaps. Discussions with industry peers, experts, and potential customers can spark ideas and uncover niche areas.

8. Geographic Considerations:

Explore geographic or regional considerations. Certain products or services may be niche in specific locations due to cultural preferences, regulatory environments, or unique local needs. Tailoring offerings to suit these geographic nuances can lead to niche market success.

9. Specialized Expertise:

Leverage specialized expertise within your team. Assess the skills, knowledge, and capabilities unique to your business. Niche opportunities often arise from leveraging specialized expertise that sets your business apart from competitors.

10. Lifestyle Changes:

Consider how societal or lifestyle changes may create new opportunities. Evolving consumer behaviors, demographics, or cultural shifts can create niche markets that were not apparent before.

11. Technology Integration:

Explore how technology can open up niche opportunities. Innovations in technology often create new markets or redefine existing ones. Assess how your business can leverage technology to meet specific needs uniquely.

12. Regulatory Changes:

Stay informed about regulatory changes that may impact your industry. New regulations can create opportunities for businesses that can adapt and innovate to meet compliance requirements or address new market demands.

In conclusion, identifying niche opportunities requires a combination of market awareness,

customer insights, and a willingness to explore
unconventional paths. By staying attuned to market
dynamics, consumer needs, and emerging trends,
businesses can position themselves to discover and
capitalize on niche opportunities that fuel growth
and differentiation.

CHAPTER 3: Financial Management Strategies

Efficient Budgeting and Resource Allocation

Efficient budgeting and resource allocation are foundational pillars of effective financial management, serving as key drivers for organizational success. A comprehensive budget is more than a financial document; it is a strategic tool that encompasses all facets of a business, from operational expenditures to capital investments and marketing initiatives. The alignment of budgeting with strategic goals ensures that financial resources are not only allocated judiciously but are also directed toward activities that contribute most effectively to the overall success and sustainability of the organization.

Flexibility is a crucial attribute in the budgeting process, recognizing the inevitability of unforeseen circumstances or changes in the business environment. A flexible budget allows for adaptability, enabling businesses to respond promptly to evolving conditions without compromising financial stability. An innovative approach to budgeting, such as zero-based budgeting, introduces a rigorous evaluation process where each budget cycle starts from zero, requiring justification for all expenses. This approach encourages a thorough examination of each line item, promoting efficiency and preventing unnecessary expenditures.

Analyzing historical financial data provides valuable insights into spending patterns, cost drivers, and areas where efficiencies can be gained. It forms the basis for informed decision-making and helps businesses identify trends that may impact future resource allocation. Cost-benefit analyses become pivotal in the budgeting process, enabling businesses to evaluate the expected return on investment for each allocation of resources. This analytical approach helps prioritize initiatives that deliver the greatest value, ensuring that resources are deployed strategically.

Contingency planning is integral to efficient budgeting, with the inclusion of reserve funds to address unexpected expenses or capitalize on unforeseen opportunities. This financial buffer serves as a risk mitigation strategy, providing the organization with the flexibility to navigate uncertainties. Regular monitoring of actual expenses against the budget is a dynamic process that requires ongoing attention. Adjustments are made as needed, ensuring that the budget remains a living document, closely aligned with the evolving needs and goals of the business.

Investing in efficiency improvements is a forward-looking strategy that pays dividends in the long run. This can involve the adoption of technology, process enhancements, and employee training, all of which contribute to long-term cost savings and improved operational performance. Resource optimization is another critical consideration, emphasizing the maximization of existing assets before seeking additional funding. This involves a thorough evaluation of current processes and assets to ensure they are utilized to their full potential.

Transparent communication about budgetary constraints and priorities across the organization is essential for fostering a collective understanding. When stakeholders, from leadership to individual contributors, are aware of the budgeting process, strategic goals, and their roles in contributing to financial objectives, it creates a cohesive and informed organizational culture.

Embracing a culture of continuous improvement is the final touchstone of efficient budgeting and resource allocation. Regular assessments of budgeting processes, seeking opportunities for refinement, and encouraging feedback from team members contribute to an environment of adaptability and optimization. Through this ongoing commitment to improvement, businesses not only enhance their financial resilience but also position themselves for sustained growth and success in the ever-evolving business landscape.

Maximizing Revenue Streams

Maximizing revenue streams is a multifaceted endeavor that involves strategic diversification and innovation. One approach is to diversify products or services, expanding the offerings to cater to a broader customer base. Tailoring these offerings to specific market segments through market segmentation ensures a targeted and customized approach. Pricing strategies, including dynamic pricing and bundling, can create value propositions that encourage customer spending. Building lasting customer relationships is pivotal, and implementing upselling strategies enhances revenue by encouraging existing customers to invest in additional products or upgraded services.

Embracing e-commerce and online sales provides opportunities to reach a wider audience, facilitated by a user-friendly website, online marketplaces, and digital marketing. Subscription models introduce recurring revenue streams and foster customer loyalty. Strategic partnerships with other businesses and collaborative efforts enable the exploration of new markets and the provision of bundled solutions. Utilizing data analytics for informed decision-making enhances marketing optimization, personalization, and identification of areas for revenue growth.

Cross-selling opportunities within product or service lineups, international expansion, and customer feedback for continuous innovation contribute to revenue maximization. Monetizing data assets and intellectual property provides alternative revenue streams, while participation in events and sponsorships can boost brand visibility and generate additional income. The dynamic interplay of these strategies enables businesses to not only optimize existing revenue sources but also uncover new and sustainable streams of income, ensuring long-term financial success.

CHAPTER 4: Marketing Mastery

Creating a Strong Brand Presence

Creating a strong brand presence is a multifaceted endeavor requiring strategic considerations. Start by clearly defining your brand identity, encompassing values, mission, and unique selling propositions. Consistency is key—ensure that your messaging aligns across all channels, fostering a cohesive and recognizable brand image. Develop distinctive visual elements, such as logos, and share an authentic brand story that resonates with your audience, forging a deeper connection.

Maintain consistent branding across online and offline platforms to build a coherent identity and instill trust. Social media platforms offer a powerful avenue for engagement; leverage them to connect with your audience, share compelling content, and humanize your brand. Prioritize a positive user experience across all touchpoints, from your website to product packaging. An effective content marketing strategy, aligned with your brand voice, establishes authority and credibility.

Encourage brand advocacy by showcasing positive customer experiences through testimonials and user-generated content. Engage in community involvement and corporate social responsibility initiatives to align your brand with positive values. Consistent quality in products or services contributes to a positive reputation, fostering repeat business and positive word-of-mouth. Actively monitor and respond to customer feedback, showcasing a commitment to satisfaction and improvement.

Investing in professional branding materials and design elevates the overall perception of your brand. Finally, create memorable brand experiences through events, promotions, or personalized interactions, contributing to positive brand associations and customer loyalty. By conscientiously implementing these strategies, businesses can cultivate a robust brand presence that resonates with their audience, fosters loyalty, and positions them as leaders in their industry.

Leveraging Digital Marketing Tools

Leveraging an extensive array of digital marketing tools is paramount for businesses seeking not only visibility but also sustained engagement and conversion in the ever-evolving digital landscape. At the core of a robust digital strategy lies Search Engine Optimization (SEO), where tools facilitate comprehensive keyword research, content optimization, and backlink building, ensuring that a website is not just present but prominently featured in search engine results.

Content marketing, a cornerstone of digital presence, is further refined through tools that streamline content creation, distribution, and analytics. Social media marketing tools, exemplified by platforms like Hootsuite or Buffer, empower businesses to efficiently manage multiple channels, allowing scheduled posts and in-depth analyses of engagement metrics.

Email marketing, a stalwart in direct communication, benefits from tools such as Mailchimp, offering capabilities for targeted campaigns, segmentation, automation, and analytics. Pay-per-click (PPC) advertising tools, exemplified by Google Ads, provide businesses with the means to run targeted campaigns across search and social media platforms, optimizing visibility to a specific audience.

Analytical tools like Google Analytics stand as indispensable assets, offering insights into website performance, user behavior, and the effectiveness of various marketing efforts. The advent of marketing automation tools, like HubSpot or Marketo, elevates efficiency by streamlining repetitive tasks, nurturing leads, and enabling personalized communication at scale.

Video marketing, a dynamic and engaging medium, utilizes platforms like YouTube or Vimeo and is supported by a suite of video creation and editing tools. Influencer marketing platforms connect brands with influencers, fostering collaborations that expand reach and resonate with specific target audiences. Chatbots and AI-powered assistants enhance customer engagement, providing instant responses to inquiries and improving overall user experience.

Remarketing tools, including Google AdWords or AdRoll, contribute to a nuanced strategy by retargeting ads to users who have previously engaged with a website. Social listening tools monitor and analyze online conversations, providing businesses with valuable insights into brand sentiment, industry trends, and opportunities for refinement.

Mobile marketing, recognizing the prevalence of mobile users, optimizes strategies for smartphones and tablets. This involves not only responsive design but also targeted advertising to ensure a seamless experience for users on diverse devices.

By integrating this comprehensive suite of digital marketing tools into their strategy, businesses can orchestrate a holistic approach to reaching, engaging, and converting their target audience. This multifaceted toolkit, aligned with strategic objectives, positions businesses to navigate the complexities of the digital landscape, fostering sustainable growth and success.

CHAPTER 5: Innovation and Adaptability

Embracing Technological Advancements

Embracing technological advancements is not merely a choice for businesses; it's a necessity in navigating the complex and rapidly evolving landscape of today's digital era. Cultivating a culture of continuous learning within the organization is foundational, encouraging employees to stay informed about the latest technological trends through training programs, workshops, and participation in industry conferences. This approach not only enhances the skill set of the workforce but also fosters adaptability, ensuring that the organization is ready to seamlessly integrate new technologies into its operations.

Staying informed about emerging technologies specific to the industry is equally crucial. Whether it's artificial intelligence, blockchain, or the Internet of Things, a proactive approach to understanding and exploring these advancements allows businesses to identify potential applications that can drive efficiency, innovation, and competitive advantage. This proactive stance often involves an investment in research and development initiatives, providing the resources needed to experiment with cutting-edge technologies, assess their feasibility, and identify innovative solutions that can propel business growth.

One of the transformative technological shifts is the integration of cloud computing. Businesses are increasingly leveraging cloud-based solutions for enhanced scalability, flexibility, and cost-effectiveness. This technology allows organizations to access and store data securely, collaborate in real-time, and deploy applications without the need for extensive on-premises infrastructure. The scalability and accessibility offered by cloud computing are particularly valuable in an environment where adaptability and responsiveness to market changes are paramount.

Data analytics tools have become indispensable for businesses seeking to extract meaningful insights from vast datasets. Informed decision-making based on these data-driven insights can optimize operations, identify trends, and enhance overall business performance. Artificial intelligence (AI) and machine learning (ML) technologies are further enhancing business processes by automating repetitive tasks, analyzing complex data patterns, and providing predictive analytics. These technologies not only increase operational efficiency but also open new possibilities in customer service, product development, and personalized user experiences.

The increasing prevalence of remote work underscores the importance of embracing collaboration tools and technologies. Video conferencing, project management platforms, and collaborative document editing tools facilitate seamless communication and teamwork, regardless of physical location. Moreover, the trend toward remote work has prompted businesses to reevaluate their technological infrastructure, placing a heightened emphasis on cybersecurity. Robust cybersecurity measures are vital to protecting sensitive data and maintaining customer trust in an era of sophisticated cyber threats.

In addition to these advancements, exploring the potential applications of blockchain technology for enhanced transparency in transactions, implementing Customer Relationship Management (CRM) systems for managing and analyzing customer interactions, and optimizing for mobile technologies further exemplify the multifaceted approach that businesses can take to fully embrace and leverage technological advancements.

In essence, businesses that proactively integrate and leverage these technological advancements position themselves not only to navigate the challenges of today's business environment but also to unlock new possibilities for growth, innovation, and sustained success in the future.

Navigating Economic Uncertainties

Navigating economic uncertainties demands a multifaceted approach from businesses, particularly in the face of unpredictable market dynamics. Employing scenario planning emerges as a key strategy, enabling businesses to anticipate various economic outcomes and develop contingency plans to respond swiftly to changing conditions. Diversification of revenue streams stands as a protective measure, reducing dependence on a singular source and enhancing overall financial stability. Agile financial management practices, including regular budget reviews, offer flexibility to reallocate resources strategically and adapt to evolving economic conditions.

Maintaining a customer-centric approach proves essential, as strong customer relationships foster loyalty even during economic challenges. Robust supply chain management involves diversifying suppliers and ensuring clear communication, reducing vulnerability to disruptions. Strategic cost management becomes imperative, involving the identification of areas for cost reduction without compromising essential functions. Embracing digital transformation enhances operational efficiency and adaptability, positioning businesses to thrive in a digital economy.

Vigilance to market trends and shifts in consumer behavior is crucial, necessitating regular assessments of the competitive landscape and proactive adaptation of strategies. Investing in talent management and reskilling initiatives ensures a workforce equipped with the skills needed in evolving economic landscapes. Collaboration with industry peers, participation in industry associations, and leveraging networking opportunities provide a supportive environment for navigating economic uncertainties.

Robust risk management strategies, including the identification and assessment of potential risks, contribute to proactive risk management. Staying informed about government policies and regulations and engaging with relevant authorities are vital for understanding potential changes and advocating for policies that support business continuity. Lastly, resilient leadership, capable of adapting to change, effective communication, and inspiring confidence, plays a pivotal role in guiding organizations through economic uncertainties. In essence, businesses adopting these strategies proactively position themselves not only to weather economic uncertainties but also to adapt, grow, and achieve long-term success.

CHAPTER 6: Leadership for Profitability

Effective Decision-making

Effective decision-making is a pivotal skill that serves as the bedrock for individual and organizational success. At its core, this process necessitates a systematic and thoughtful approach to discern the best course of action amid various alternatives. Adopting a data-driven mindset forms a fundamental principle, emphasizing the importance of basing decisions on reliable information to ensure objectivity and alignment with organizational goals. Clarity of objectives is equally crucial, requiring a well-defined purpose to maintain focus and alignment with broader strategies.

The consideration of alternatives involves a comprehensive evaluation of options, weighing their pros and cons to make informed choices. Stakeholder involvement adds depth to decision-making, acknowledging the perspectives of those affected and fostering inclusivity. A critical step involves assessing the risks and benefits associated with each option, ensuring a thorough understanding of potential outcomes.

Utilizing decision-making models or frameworks, such as SWOT analysis, provides a structured approach to systematically assess options. Recognizing the importance of timing underscores the need for prompt action when required, balancing the need for thorough analysis with timely execution. Establishing accountability and responsibility ensures a culture of ownership, while flexibility and adaptability acknowledge the dynamic nature of situations.

Continuous learning and feedback treat decisions as opportunities for improvement, using feedback to refine the decision-making process. Ethical considerations guide decision-makers to uphold organizational values and maintain trust. Developing emotional intelligence becomes crucial for navigating the human aspects of decision-making, and fostering effective communication and collaboration.

Reflecting on past decisions serves as a learning mechanism, allowing for the analysis of contributing factors to success or challenges. In essence, effective decision-making amalgamates analytical prowess, collaboration, and adaptability. By embracing these principles, individuals and organizations can fortify their capacity to make strategic, well-informed decisions that align with their objectives and contribute to sustained success.

Building and Leading High-performing Teams

Building and leading high-performing teams is a complex endeavor that demands a strategic and people-centric approach. It starts with establishing a clear vision and goals, ensuring that every team member comprehends the collective purpose and direction. Strategic recruitment plays a pivotal role, as assembling a diverse set of skills and strengths contributes to a well-rounded team dynamic. Open communication is fundamental, creating an environment where team members feel empowered to express ideas, concerns, and feedback.

Clearly defined roles and responsibilities foster accountability, ensuring that each team member understands their contributions to the overarching objectives. Encouraging collaboration is key, promoting a culture where collective efforts drive success through brainstorming sessions, cross-functional collaboration, and knowledge sharing. Providing necessary resources and support, including professional development opportunities and a positive work environment, is essential for team success.

Empowering and trusting team members with responsibilities builds confidence and a sense of ownership. Continuous feedback mechanisms, such as regular performance reviews and constructive feedback, contribute to ongoing professional development. Adaptability and flexibility are crucial in the face of changing circumstances, fostering resilience within the team.

Leading by example sets the tone for the team, exemplifying values, work ethic, and a commitment to continuous improvement. Conflict resolution processes, when implemented promptly and constructively, contribute to maintaining a harmonious team environment. Investing in professional development and celebrating diversity further enriches the team, fostering innovation and problem-solving.

In essence, the art of building and leading high-performing teams involves a delicate balance of strategic planning, effective communication, and a deep understanding of the individuals who comprise the team. By integrating these principles, leaders can cultivate a culture of collaboration, excellence, and shared commitment that propels the team towards achieving organizational goals.

CHAPTER 7: Case Studies of Economic Triumphs

Successful Businesses and their Strategies

Successful businesses share common strategies that contribute to their sustained growth and prominence. First and foremost, they articulate a clear vision and mission, providing a guiding purpose that aligns efforts toward a common goal. Customer-centric focus is paramount, with a dedication to understanding customer needs, delivering exceptional value, and fostering long-term relationships. Adaptability and innovation are key characteristics, as successful businesses continuously evolve to meet the dynamic demands of the market.

Effective leadership is foundational, with visionary and adaptable leaders inspiring teams, cultivating positive cultures, and making strategic decisions. Robust marketing and branding strategies enhance visibility and brand recognition, creating compelling narratives that resonate with the target audience. Operational efficiency is a priority, with

successful businesses streamlining processes to
enhance productivity and reduce costs.

Delivering high-quality products or services
builds trust and loyalty, while strategic partnerships
open new avenues for growth. Prudent financial
management, a focus on employee engagement and
development, and data-driven decision-making
contribute to overall success. Actively seeking
customer feedback and incorporating it into
continuous improvement processes is a hallmark of
customer-centric businesses.

Embracing social responsibility and sustainability
practices enhances brand reputation, and successful
businesses integrate ethical and sustainable practices
into their operations. Calculated risk-taking, focus
on long-term goals, and a commitment to excellence
contribute to sustained growth and resilience.
Through a combination of these strategies,
successful businesses navigate challenges, capitalize
on opportunities, and establish themselves as leaders
in their industries.

Lessons Learned from Notable Economic Successes

Notable economic successes offer valuable lessons that extend beyond individual nations, providing insights applicable to diverse contexts. One key lesson underscores the importance of diversifying the economy, reducing dependence on a single sector to enhance resilience. Education and workforce development emerge as crucial contributors to success, emphasizing the significance of cultivating a skilled and knowledgeable workforce. Innovation and technological advancements play a central role, showcasing the necessity of investing in research and development to foster economic growth.

Investment in robust infrastructure is a recurring theme, as it creates an environment conducive to business development and operational efficiency. Successful economies recognize the benefits of openness to global trade, leveraging international markets for growth and specialization. The implementation of sound fiscal and monetary policies is critical, ensuring macroeconomic stability and responsible financial management. Entrepreneurship and small business support are pivotal for economic dynamism, contributing to vibrant entrepreneurial ecosystems.

Prioritizing social and environmental responsibility aligns with the evolving understanding of sustainable economic success. Inclusive growth strategies, which address income inequality and promote social mobility, contribute to a more stable and equitable economic landscape. Strong institutions and the rule of law are foundational, fostering transparent and effective legal systems that support business and investment. Long-term planning, vision, adaptability, and resilience collectively underscore the importance of sustained efforts in navigating economic challenges and pursuing lasting success. These lessons serve as guiding principles for nations and businesses aiming to cultivate growth, competitiveness, and a resilient economic foundation.

CHAPTER 8: Challenges and Solutions

Common Obstacles to Economic Triumph

Achieving economic triumph is often impeded by common obstacles that nations and businesses must navigate. Economic inequality stands out as a formidable challenge, hindering progress by limiting access to opportunities and resources. Additionally, a lack of access to quality education hampers human capital development, constraining workforce potential and innovation. Political instability can disrupt economic activities, creating an uncertain environment that deters investments and erodes confidence.

Corruption poses a significant barrier, undermining the rule of law and distorting market mechanisms. Inadequate infrastructure, insufficient access to capital, and global economic uncertainties further compound challenges, impacting business operations and economic prospects. Environmental degradation and insufficient sustainability practices pose threats to long-term success, requiring a delicate balance between economic development and environmental responsibility.

Technological disruptions and trade barriers can also impede economic growth, necessitating adaptability and open trade policies. Demographic challenges, lack of innovation culture, and weak adherence to the rule of law are additional obstacles that demand strategic solutions. Overcoming these barriers requires a holistic and collaborative approach, involving governments, businesses, and society to implement policies, investments, and practices that foster inclusivity, sustainability, and resilience in the face of complex economic challenges.

Insufficient access to capital, especially for small and medium-sized enterprises (SMEs), represents a critical hurdle for entrepreneurship and business expansion. Global economic uncertainties, often driven by factors beyond national control, can have profound impacts on economic trajectories. These uncertainties include economic downturns in major markets or geopolitical tensions that influence trade dynamics and market conditions. Environmental challenges, such as climate change and resource depletion, necessitate sustainable practices for long-term economic viability.

Moreover, demographic challenges, including aging populations or imbalances, can strain social welfare systems and impact workforce productivity. Lack of innovation culture and inadequate investment in research and development hinder a nation's ability to stay competitive in a rapidly evolving global economy. Weak legal frameworks and a lack of adherence to the rule of law create an unstable business environment, deterring investments and hindering economic progress.

Addressing these obstacles requires strategic and coordinated efforts. Governments need to implement policies that promote inclusivity, education, innovation, and sustainability. Businesses must adopt practices that prioritize ethical conduct, environmental responsibility, and long-term viability. Collaboration between public and private sectors, along with a commitment to addressing systemic issues like corruption and inequality, is essential for overcoming these obstacles and fostering an environment conducive to sustained economic triumph.

Proven Solutions and Strategies

Proven solutions and strategies have emerged as effective means to overcome common obstacles and foster economic triumph. Inclusive economic policies, addressing issues of inequality and promoting equal opportunities, stand out as foundational. Investing in education and workforce development remains pivotal, contributing to a skilled workforce that fuels innovation and productivity. Good governance and robust anti-corruption measures create transparent business environments, enhancing investor confidence and supporting sustainable development.

Infrastructure development, including investments in transportation, energy, and technology, plays a critical role in improving overall business efficiency and competitiveness. Ensuring access to capital, particularly for small and medium-sized enterprises, stimulates entrepreneurship and business expansion. Embracing global trade partnerships opens avenues for growth, while sustainable practices balance economic development with environmental responsibility.

Encouraging technological adoption and fostering innovation cultures contribute to competitiveness in a rapidly evolving landscape. Social responsibility initiatives, encompassing ethical conduct and community engagement, enhance brand reputation and contribute to positive business environments. Legal and judicial reforms strengthen the foundations of a secure business environment, attracting investments.

Adaptive economic policies that respond to global and local challenges are crucial, allowing for flexibility in navigating changing economic conditions. Collaboration between the public and private sectors, through initiatives like public-private partnerships, facilitates comprehensive solutions by combining resources and expertise. By applying these proven solutions and strategies, nations and businesses can effectively overcome obstacles, promote sustainable growth, and create environments conducive to long-term economic triumph.

Continuing on the path of proven solutions and strategies for economic triumph, social responsibility initiatives have gained prominence. Companies that prioritize ethical conduct, community engagement, and social impact often foster a positive business environment, contributing to long-term success. This commitment to social responsibility not only enhances brand reputation but also aligns businesses with societal values.

Legal and judicial reforms play a pivotal role in creating a secure business environment. Clear and enforceable legal frameworks attract investments, provide a foundation for economic growth, and contribute to a stable and predictable business climate. Adaptive economic policies, capable of responding to dynamic global and local challenges, showcase a government's agility and foresight, fostering resilience against economic uncertainties.

Collaboration between sectors, particularly through public-private partnerships, has proven effective in addressing complex challenges. By combining the resources and expertise of both public and private entities, comprehensive solutions can be crafted to navigate multifaceted obstacles. This collaborative approach ensures that diverse perspectives and capabilities are harnessed to achieve shared economic goals.

In conclusion, these proven solutions form a multifaceted toolkit for nations and businesses aspiring to achieve economic triumph. Their successful implementation hinges on a holistic and collaborative approach, underlining the interconnectedness of economic, social, and environmental factors. As stakeholders converge on these strategies, they pave the way for sustainable growth, resilience, and prosperity in the face of a rapidly evolving global landscape.

CHAPTER 9: Future Trends in Profit Prowess

Emerging Opportunities in the Global Economy

Emerging opportunities are reshaping the global economy, offering avenues for growth and innovation. One significant area is the surge in green and sustainable technologies, with a focus on renewable energy, sustainable agriculture, and eco-friendly manufacturing. The ongoing digital transformation presents opportunities for businesses adopting technologies like artificial intelligence, blockchain, and the Internet of Things, enhancing efficiency and competitiveness. The rise of e-commerce and digital services is evident, driven by changing consumer behaviors and preferences, providing significant growth prospects.

Healthcare innovation, including telemedicine and personalized medicine, is transforming the healthcare sector. Remote work has catalyzed opportunities in collaboration tools and virtual communication platforms as businesses adapt to evolving work trends. Sustainable finance and impact investing are gaining traction, reflecting a growing interest in socially responsible and environmentally friendly investment opportunities. Biotechnology and life sciences are witnessing breakthroughs in genetic engineering, precision medicine, and biopharmaceuticals.

Renewable energy and energy storage are pivotal in the global transition towards sustainable energy sources. Cybersecurity has become a critical focus as digital connectivity expands, creating opportunities for companies providing cybersecurity solutions. Circular economy practices emphasizing recycling and sustainable consumption are gaining popularity, offering opportunities for businesses aligning with these principles. The electric vehicle industry is thriving, with opportunities in EV manufacturing, charging infrastructure, and sustainable transportation solutions.

Data analytics and artificial intelligence play a crucial role in decision-making as businesses leverage data-driven insights for operational efficiency and strategic planning. Embracing these emerging opportunities requires adaptability, innovation, and a deep understanding of market dynamics. Companies and entrepreneurs positioned to capitalize on these evolving sectors contribute to

the dynamic landscape of the global economy,
driving positive change and sustainable growth.

Adapting to Future Economic Landscapes

Adapting to future economic landscapes demands a proactive and strategic approach. Businesses must prioritize digital transformation, leveraging technologies like automation and artificial intelligence to enhance agility and competitiveness. Fostering a culture of innovation and investing in research and development are essential for staying ahead in evolving industries. Building resilient supply chains, diversifying suppliers, and implementing risk management strategies are critical to withstand disruptions.

Sustainability should be integrated into business practices, aligning with growing consumer and investor preferences for environmentally conscious choices. Investment in education and workforce development is crucial to address the changing skills landscape, promoting lifelong learning and upskilling programs. Global collaboration is paramount to tackle shared challenges, fostering innovation and solutions on an international scale.

Strengthening cybersecurity measures is imperative as digital reliance increases, safeguarding sensitive information and maintaining trust in digital interactions. Embracing remote work and flexible employment models is a key adaptation to the changing nature of work, supported by effective remote collaboration technologies. Recognizing the importance of health and well-being in the workforce involves implementing wellness programs and creating a culture that values the holistic well-being of employees.

Diversifying economies reduces reliance on a single sector, enhancing economic resilience. Anticipating demographic changes and planning for an aging population ensures policies and infrastructure support evolving workforce needs. Regulatory agility is crucial to adapt to changing business landscapes, encouraging innovation while maintaining ethical practices. Addressing social inequities is paramount for fostering inclusivity and stability in society.

Staying informed about global economic trends and maintaining adaptability are fundamental. Continuous monitoring allows for informed decision-making in dynamic environments, positioning individuals, businesses, and nations to thrive in the unfolding economic landscape.

CONCLUSION

Adapting to the intricacies of future economic landscapes necessitates a nuanced and comprehensive approach that spans various facets of individual, business, and national strategies. A pivotal aspect is the relentless pursuit of digital transformation. Individuals and organizations alike must embrace emerging technologies, from automation to artificial intelligence, to fortify their agility and competitiveness in an increasingly digitized world. Concurrently, fostering a culture of innovation and committing to robust research and development efforts are foundational. This ensures the continuous evolution of industries and the maintenance of a competitive edge in the face of technological advancements.

The establishment of resilient supply chains is crucial for mitigating disruptions, with strategies including supplier diversification, risk management protocols, and the integration of real-time visibility technologies. Sustainability is not just an ethical consideration but a strategic imperative. Businesses must integrate sustainable practices into their core operations to align with the growing preferences of consumers and investors for environmentally conscious choices. Simultaneously, investments in education and workforce development are imperative to address the swiftly changing skills landscape. Encouraging lifelong learning and upskilling programs ensures individuals and the workforce remain adaptable and competitive.

Global collaboration emerges as an essential theme. In a world interconnected by digital threads, international cooperation becomes crucial for addressing shared challenges and fostering innovation on a global scale. Robust cybersecurity measures are imperative to safeguard sensitive information and maintain trust in digital interactions, particularly as dependence on digital platforms grows.

The shift towards remote work and flexible employment models necessitates comprehensive adaptation. Businesses should leverage technologies that support effective remote collaboration, and policies should be crafted to accommodate changing work dynamics. Prioritizing health and well-being in the workforce, encompassing wellness programs and a culture that values holistic well-being, contributes not only to employee satisfaction but also to sustained productivity.

Diversification of economies is vital for resilience. Over-reliance on a single sector can render economies vulnerable to fluctuations. Anticipating demographic changes, particularly an aging population, calls for strategic planning in policies and infrastructure to support evolving workforce needs. Regulatory agility is indispensable, striking a balance between fostering innovation and ensuring responsible business practices.

Addressing social inequities becomes a foundational element for creating a stable and inclusive society. Promoting diversity and equal access to opportunities contributes to societal cohesion and economic stability. Continuous monitoring of global economic trends and a commitment to adaptability are critical for making informed decisions in dynamic environments. By weaving these multifaceted strategies into their fabric, individuals, businesses, and nations can not only adapt to but also thrive in the unfolding economic landscape, positioning themselves for sustained success amid evolving challenges and opportunities.

Embarking on the journey towards economic triumph is a commendable pursuit that requires resilience, vision, and unwavering determination. As you navigate the intricate landscape of economic endeavors, remember that challenges are not obstacles but stepping stones to growth and innovation. Embrace each hurdle as an opportunity to learn, adapt, and refine your strategies.

In the face of uncertainties, maintain a forward-looking perspective. Your ability to anticipate and adapt to changes will be a cornerstone of your success. Stay informed about global trends, emerging opportunities, and evolving consumer behaviors. In the dynamic world of economics, those who remain agile and forward-thinking often find themselves at the forefront of innovation.

Surround yourself with a network of mentors, collaborators, and like-minded individuals. The exchange of ideas and experiences can be a powerful catalyst for growth. Seek inspiration from those who have navigated similar paths, learning from both their successes and setbacks. Remember, collaboration often amplifies creativity and resilience.

Celebrate small victories along the way. Economic triumph is often a culmination of incremental successes. Recognize and appreciate the progress you make, no matter how small. This mindset not only fuels motivation but also provides a clearer perspective on the journey ahead.

Embrace a culture of continuous learning. The economic landscape is ever-evolving, and staying at the forefront requires a commitment to acquiring new knowledge and skills. Embrace challenges as opportunities to expand your expertise and develop a versatile skill set.

Finally, maintain a steadfast belief in your vision. Economic triumph is not solely about financial gains but also about creating positive impact and contributing to the greater good. Your dedication to a purpose-driven approach will not only propel you forward but also resonate with stakeholders who share your values.

In the pursuit of economic triumph, remember that setbacks are not defeats but valuable lessons. Stay focused on your goals, adapt to change with resilience, and let your passion drive you forward. The path to economic success is challenging, but with dedication and a forward-looking mindset, you have the potential to shape a future of prosperity and impact.